# Sonata No. 1
## for Flute and Piano
### *To Jeanne Baxtresser*

I

Eugénie R. Rocherolle

# SONATA NO. 1
## FOR FLUTE AND PIANO

EUGÉNIE R. ROCHEROLLE

_____

## FLUTE PART

_____

ISBN 978-1-4234-8796-8

HAL•LEONARD®
CORPORATION
7777 W. BLUEMOUND RD. P.O. BOX 13819 MILWAUKEE, WI 53213

www.halleonard.com

(This page has been left blank to facilitate page turns.)

## II

# III

mosso ( ♩ = 120)